# A Call to PRAY

30 day Experience
Vol. 7

# PRAYER JOURNAL

# A Call to PRAY

## PRAYER JOURNAL

Published by Krystal Lee Enterprises (KLE Publishing)
Copyright © 2026 by K. Lee All rights reserved. Please
send comments and questions:

Krystal Lee Enterprises
770-240-0089 Ext. 1
sales@KLEPub.com

To Reach the Author:
Email: me@authorklee.com or me@drkrystallee.com

Web: www.AuthorKLee.com
Social Handle: AuthorKLee on all pages
FB, IG, Tiktok, Twitter (X), Pinterest, LinkedIn, YouTube

ISBN: **979-8-89987-921-0**

# DEDICATION

This book is dedicated to those who believe or pray that prayer can change their situation. This book serves as a reminder that prayer changes things and is the answer to whatever you are facing now. May you be encouraged by the power of this series to change the world through the Living Power of Yah, God Almighty.

Thank you to each and every one of you who are supporting this series through prayer, buying books/ebooks, sharing books/ebooks, or sponsoring events. A sincere thank you from the bottom of my heart is extended, which only my humble words hope to demonstrate.

To my family and close friends, thank you for supporting this book! To my husband, I love you; to my children, I love each and every one of you.

The best is First and Last, Alpha and Omega, to my life and heart. To my Lord and Savior, Yahshua, thank you for all the gifts you have given me and continue to give me on a daily basis. Words cannot express all of my gratitude. If you don't know Him, please meet Him and let your world change. I am a witness of His continued goodness.

# A Call to PRAY

## PRAYER JOURNAL

Table of Contents

Table of Contents Continued

Table of Contents Continued

# A Call to PRAY

K. Lee

day Experience
Vol. 1 - 12

## Thank You!

If you haven't purchased a book from the series, please consider buying one copy and get access to all 12 digital copies as soon as they release! Get all 12 books, and get the audiobooks and digital books free!

Visit or Scan: AuthorKLee.com

For every 250 copies sold, we can publish the next book in the series. My goal is to publish all 12 within a calendar year and translate the book into 5 languages by year two. urchase your book today, or download the free digital copies to support this series and share, please!

# INTRODUCTION

In my life as a chaplain, I am a witness to the power of prayer. If you look at prayer as a means to get what you want from God, Yah, or somebody. You might want to rethink the purpose and importance of prayer. As an ordained chaplain and minister, believer and mother, friend and business owner, I am *Called to Pray*.

This book is a dedication to the power of prayer and its ability to reach heaven. I thank Yah for His Word and desire to speak with us, His creation. It is through prayer that we spend time and get to know the Father as our Lord and Savior.

He loves us and wants us to come to Him with our emotions, will, and for our thoughts to include Him. Whether you are facing challenges or success, feeling love or pain, hopeful or depressed, this book series of featured prayers will touch and agree with the prayers of the righteous or those seeking rest, peace, or help to petition Yahweh, the only true God, for direction and resolution.

The first prayer we have to recite is the Lord's Prayer, which is available in Vol. 1 of this series, but will be included in this book as well as every book in the series. There are topics in each book that will make you want the entire 12-book collection.

So consider grabbing all 12 and get a special gift! Scan the QR and order. We have a goal to sell 250 bundles of 12 to support the publication of all books. As a thanks, I will give you 5 digital series to give away to friends or family members, plus give you a personally signed thank you letter and gift pack for your help and commitment.

Here is a short list of additional topics before the 30 entries of prayer.

Vol. 1 Salvation

Vol. 2 Forgiveness and Debt Cancellation

Vol. 3 The Sabbath

Vol. 4 Fasting and Praying

Vol. 5 Fruits of the Spirit

Vol. 6 Love Conquers All

Vol. 7 Beatitudes

This series will gently but firmly hold your hand so you are not afraid to face tomorrow and whatever the rain might bring. It rains on the just and the unjust, so don't feel that the events happening are a direct fault of your own. Allow this book and the entire series to lift your spirit.

Something you should know about prayer to help ease your nerves or feelings of inadequacy. The Lord's Prayer was the example given to us by the Messiah for how to pray in the Bible. Prayer doesn't have to be long, but at times it is. Prayer doesn't have to sound great or use catchy phrases, but it can. It needs to be an open conversation with your heart in the right place with God Almighty. Allow your heart to fill with hope as you pray and visualize what can be–even if it is only for a little bit. God can work with that and surely bring peace to your life.

Real quick, before we pray, if you are wondering how to look up the citations in this book or the scriptures in parentheses, here is how to find the verse for further exploration. For example, 1 Corinthians 12:27. The name of the book is mentioned first. In this case, 1 Corinthians. There are two books, 1 Corinthians and 2 Corinthians, in the Bible. The first number before the ":" is the chapter. Here, we would go to chapter 12. Then the last number references the verse or series of verses. Here it would be verse 27, but if you see 12-27, then it would be verses 12 through 27.

In your Bible, phone, or tablet, go to Matthew 6:9-13 and let's read the Lord's Prayer together aloud.

Pray then like this:

"Our Father in heaven,
hallowed be Your name.

Your kingdom come,
Your will be done,
  on earth as it is in heaven.

Give us this day our daily bread,

and forgive us our debts,
as we also have forgiven our debtors.

And lead us not into temptation,
but deliver us from evil."

We believe that our Father is above the earth and capable of addressing all of our problems. We know that His desire is to bring His Kingdom, the Kingdom of God, to earth. Yahshua (Jesus) preached about the Kingdom of God. We lean on Yah to provide us with our needs because we know that we don't live off bread alone, but every Word from God (Matthew 4:4).

This prayer reminds us of the importance of forgiving those who hurt us so we too can be forgiving. This is a request to keep us from becoming the very thing that hurt us. It is tempting to live a life of sin and to do things to please our own ideas, appetites, and desires. We ask the Father to help us not put our thoughts and emotions above His thoughts. His thoughts are not ours but higher (Isaiah 55:8-9).

So as Matthew 6:14-15 reads, "For if you forgive others their trespasses, your heavenly Father will also forgive you, 15 but if you do not forgive others their trespasses, neither will your Father forgive your trespasses." We must be examples of His goodness and forgiveness. We need to be open to His lead on how to respond to events in our lives.

If the Father above the Heavens is not your Lord and His Son, Yahshua Jesus the Christ, not your Savior, I want you to go to Vol. 1 of this series and read the introduction section to understand salvation and what it means to give your life to Christ. It is a total life commitment, and I want you to pray a salvation prayer with your whole heart, knowing what you are surrendering and what you will receive.

I want you to know what it means to be forgiven of your sins or trespasses, so you have the confidence and will to forgive others. It can be hard to forgive others when you don't see how you, too, benefited from forgiveness. Understanding what Sin is, the 10 Commandments are part of it, the 7 Abominations, and the 7 Deadly Sins all point to it. But it is so much more that the Father does for us than redeem us from these things.

I encourage you to read Volumes 1 and 2 to learn more about salvation and forgiveness, and in 3, the power of The Sabbath, but in 4, the reason why we fast and pray. In Volume 5, I wanted to review the fruits of the Spirit, in Volume 6, how LOVE conquers all, and finally in this one, the Beatitudes.

# Beatitudes

Matthew Chapter 5 in the Bible is a good foundation for the uniqueness and the calling on a believer's life. We are not just the children of Yahweh, God Almighty; we are joint heirs with Christ, and we have a role in the earth. I know we can think we are just people, but you are a Kingdom Citizen in the Kingdom of God. We are ambassadors who point to the Kingdom of God, and our role is to help people obtain citizenship by showing them the way.

To understand the beatitudes, I want to first review the parable of being the salt of the earth. After the beatitudes in the Bible, Christ talks about being the salt of the earth. He says in Matthew 5 beginning at verse 3:

> "You are the salt of the earth, but if salt has lost its taste, how shall its saltiness be restored? It is no longer good for anything except to be thrown out and trampled under people's feet.
>
> 14 You are the light of the world. A city set on a hill cannot be hidden. 15 Nor do people light a lamp and put it under a basket, but on a stand, and it gives light to all in the house. 16 In the same way, let your light shine before others, so that they may see your good works and give glory to your Father who is in heaven."

We are not on the earth to serve ourselves. When Christ came to earth, He was not sent to be worshiped, but was sent to serve and point others to the Kingdom of God. He was sent with the assignment to show us how to live here on earth and how to be a kingdom citizen in the earth. We are told we are in the world but not of the world in John 17:15-16. We are to be the salt of the earth, which is a natural source that has a function to be salty. If we are to impact others, we have to know that our saltiness is from the Father. He gives us salt, and if we are to salt the earth, we are to function how salt does.

Salt is a preserver. Before there were refrigerators and freezers, we would salt meat to preserve it. Salt flavors, it is in saline, it is in the ocean, it is in our tears, our sweat, and throughout the earth. Salt has a purpose, and you do too. You are to be a lamp, the light in a dark and fallen world. We are to point to hope and a future that is better than our current condition. We are to bring joy to the world, as the good song says, with the healing message of Christ our Savior.

So how do we reflect the message of Christ in the earth? We have to be doers of the beatitudes to help those who can't see, to see. Those who want to know God, Yahweh, they meet Him through seeing His character in us. If we want to be examples of Christ, followers of Him, disciples, we must follow the beatitudes in our lives.

So what are they? The Messiah, Yahshua (Jesus), taught the crowd this as they gathered and sat to learn at his feet. He describes what it means to be a follower of Christ, a kingdom citizen, salt in the earth, and a lamp intended to be on a stand to shine before the nations. He says in red text in Matthew Chapter 5,

"Seeing the crowds, he went up on the mountain, and when he sat down, his disciples came to him. 2 And he opened his mouth and taught them, saying:

3 "Blessed are the poor in spirit, for theirs is the kingdom of heaven.

4 "Blessed are those who mourn, for they shall be comforted.

5 "Blessed are the meek, for they shall inherit the earth.

6 "Blessed are those who hunger and thirst for righteousness, for they shall be satisfied.

7 "Blessed are the merciful, for they shall receive mercy.

8 "Blessed are the pure in heart, for they shall see God.

9 "Blessed are the peacemakers, for they shall be called sons of God.

10 "Blessed are those who are persecuted for righteousness' sake, for theirs is the king-

dom of heaven.

11 "Blessed are you when others revile you and persecute you and utter all kinds of evil against you falsely on my account. 12 Rejoice and be glad, for your reward is great in heaven, for so they persecuted the prophets who were before you.

When we feel left alone and isolated because we are different in this world, being a reflection of God. We can take courage because we will inherit the Kingdom of God, where we all are of one mindset. For the many who have cried and mourned, like the Messiah has also, we will be comforted in knowing God will never leave nor forsake us!

We are to be meek, humble, because this allows us to serve all. We have our pride in check and we can see the value and love in everyone. We will inherit the earth because it belongs to our Father and He gives it to us to have dominion. When a good royal rules the land, the people rejoice and prosper, but when an evil one does, the people groan (Proverbs 29:2).

Blessed are those who thirst for righteousness, to do right by people and Yah, because they will be satisfied with peace. Peace that they tried to do all that they needed and should do. They are at peace knowing they are in right standing with God and blameless before men, as we are told to be (Philippians 2:15).

We are to have mercy with others and be understanding to forgive because we are recipients of it. With the parable of the king who forgave a man of his debts, who then did not forgive the debts of those who owed him with mercy, the king made him pay it in full as a judgment for him not having mercy (Matthew 18:23-35).

We are to be pure in heart and have confidence that we can be because our Father is the supplier of our needs. We don't have to rob, steal, cheat, or do underhanded things because we know that people are not our source; Yah is. He will open doors and set us on a course to win in life.

For those of us who will be persecuted for righteousness' sake, we can be encouraged. They killed the Messiah not because He sinned, but because he was against powers and systems that be. He was willing to stand up for people and their rights to live and be free according to scripture. The Kingdom of Heaven is an awareness and not just a place. Church is our sanctuary where we can be ourselves and embrace those on this journey with us, no matter their nationality, culture, language, race, or financial background.

Don't worry, still when people talk about you, lie on you, and try to make you out to be something you are not. The father will avenge us and reward us for our good works. The Messiah went through the trial and suffered the Cross, and the Good Lord turned it all to the good of humanity. So don't regret your decision to commit your Life to the Word and being a living sacrifice set apart to worship God (Yah) in how you live. Be bold and confident in your choice, knowing you have a comforter and someone who loves you.

If you don't know the healing message of Christ and what He gave to cover our sins, the salvation prayer is the route for life transformation. The Lord's Prayer or any prayer is a reminder to remain committed to the values of God and implement His standards over our own. This is arguably one of the most important prayers we can recite as a believer, the Lord's Prayer. When we are not saved and a child of God—birthed to be a new creature, the best prayer we should consider lifting up to Yahweh is the prayer of salvation.

The salvation prayer is an experience and not a checklist. It is a commitment and one that should not be taken lightly. This is a prayer that will commit your life to be subject to the rulership of the Word of God, and anything that rises up against the Word of Truth, you must condemn through love (2 Corinthians 10:5). This scripture reads, "We destroy arguments and every lofty opinion raised against the knowledge of God, and take every thought captive to obey Christ."

You will become a new creature, and the old things will pass away (2 Corinthians 5:17). And this scripture reads, "Therefore, if anyone is in Christ, he is a new creation. The old has passed away; behold, the new has come." This prayer is life-transforming, and you will go through an experience. Some will love the change Yahshua (Jesus) will bring to your life, and others will not like it, because sadly, they too don't like the Word of God.

Praying this prayer is soul transformation. That is subjecting your Mind, your Will, and your Emotions to the rulership of Christ. This further means the Word of God because Christ is the Word made into flesh. Yahshua is the atonement, when he gave his life on the cross, to restore us from a life of sin to everlasting life.

He makes us royalty in the eyes of God, a peculiar people made royalty (1 Peter 2:9). If you don't have the healing message of what sin is and what He has redeemed you from, please read Vol. 1, the Introduction, for a clear and convicting understanding that is easy to feel the love of Christ. This is about love and not hate. Freedom and not bondage.

I want you to know that it is okay if people won't like how you change. Don't be afraid.

Don't stop your journey if you are rejected by family, friends, or others you care about. You have a family that is here for you, and this is the Body of Christ (1 Corinthians 12:12-27), the unit that is the Church (1 Corinthians 12:27). You become a Child of God because you believe and love God, and are now called by His Name.

I know this is a lot, so I encourage you to find a home church that is filled with the power, the Spirit, and the Love of God to disciple you and help you grow. This book will help you to pray and welcome your Lord and Savior to areas of your life that need transformation. This is the start of your road, but it will be glorious because Yah will complete the great work He started in you (Philippians 1:6).

Allow these two verses to inspire you, Philippians 1:6, "And I am sure of this, that he who began a good work in you will bring it to completion at the day of Jesus Christ." Another good verse you must know is Deuteronomy

31:8, "It is the Lord who goes before you. He will be with you; he will not leave you or forsake you. Do not fear or be dismayed."

Alright, if you are ready to change your life and welcome THE God of all creation to enter your life through the Word of God, His Son, who died on the cross to pay for the sins of the world (More on this in Vol. 10), who was given as a gift from Yahweh to reconnect us to Him after the fall of Adam, I invite you to walk with me through the prayer of salvation.

Scan QR or visit ACallToPraySeries.com to hear the salvation prayer and get other resources.

"Father, I thank you for impressing your truth on the heart of "Say Your Name." I thank you for allowing one who was lost to become found today, and in this moment." Now, repeat after me.

"Father, I come to you because I need you. I need you to save me from the mistakes I made and the sins I have committed against You. I ask that You forgive me for the sins that I have (list your sins). Show me the right way to live my life. I confess that Yahshua is the Son of God, that He died on the cross for my sins, rose from the dead, and sits at the Right Hand of the Father. I trust that the Word is sufficient to direct my life, and I will commit to submit my thoughts and perception of the world through Your Word. I ask You to come into my life to be my Lord and Savior. I thank You for making me a new creation, in Yahshua's name, Hallelujah, and so be it!"

If you want to rededicate your life to Christ, please read this prayer:

"Father, You know me. It is not that You have left me, but I have left You. I return this day and recommit my life to You. I want You to redirect me from the ways and the cares that have me weighed down. Renew in me Your Spirit. Cleanse me, cleanse my soul, and help me to reform my mind, my heart, my body, and my will. Help me to humble myself and remain this way all the days of my life. Teach me how to continue to love You and always have a thirst for You. Thank You for redeeming me and allowing me to return to You. In Yahshua's name, hallelujah, and so be it."

**Now,** welcome to a series I titled, "A Call to Pray." In using this book series of 12 volumes, you can search the topic and find the right prayer to help you pray for where you need Yahweh to show up in your life or those you love. If you are not saved, or they are not saved, may the prayers of the righteous avail much (James 5:16). May these prayers work for you, your family, and the situations in your life. Please know, there are some prayers that need to be made through your relationship with Yahweh. He wants to know you and for you to surrender to His will, or the person you are praying for.

Others can join with you, but you will eventually need to establish your own prayer connection with the Savior, the Living Word, to see the healing power and works of His hands. As believers, we are ambassadors for Christ, but we are not saving, healing, or doing anything apart from Him, but through Him (2 Corinthians 5:20, Philippians 4:13).

Shalom, peace and blessings.

Dr. Krystal Lee

## PRAYER DECOYS

We all have something and someone we can need or look for. We may think that we have all the parts to a situation, and the person or situation looking us in the face is the answer to our prayers or our needs. If you have found that what you need is not what you have gotten too often in life, I want to encourage you to pray against decoys.

"Father, You say that we can cast our burdens on You because You care about us. Today, we are coming to You because You are all-knowing, mighty, and strong. You know what we need and how we need to move to be in alignment with Your plans for our lives. Father, today, I want to submit to You my plans, my hopes, and my dreams.

You said, not to lean on my own understanding, but to ask You, to come to You, boldly, and tell You the things I need, I care about, I desire, and I want. I submit these things to

You because I know You know better than me what is best. Father, You say Your ways are higher than man's, and we believe You. If I am getting ahead of myself, or growing anxious for having what I want, and that is blocking me from giving You what You want from me, slow me down.

Open my eyes, help me to discern the spirit, situation, and if I am acting on my own lust or desires, regardless of Your direction for my life, please forgive me. Father, You say to be a living sacrifice is my reasonable service. If I ever forget, thank You for allowing me to humble myself here at Your feet. I trust You with my life, my hopes, and my dreams. You will never leave me nor forsake me, but direct me in all my ways.

For the decoys sent to distract me, or to discourage me, I thank You for canceling the plans of the enemy to succeed in my life. May the plan be exposed, and You give me beauty for ashes. May You restore whatever I lost, and redeem whatever was taken. I thank You for opening my eyes and slowing me down so I can hear, see, and move with purpose, because I know what the real thing is. And the real is what You have for me. It is in the name of Your Son, our Lord and Savior, that we say, Hallelujah and so be it."

## Share Your Thoughts or Answered Prayers

_____

_____

_____

_____

_____

_____

_____

_____

_____

_____

_____

_____

_____

_____

_____

_____

_____

_____

_____

_____

# PRAYER GOOD

If you are needing a good thing in your life, this prayer is for you. Good is who God is, and for some of us, we have never had it. We are used to less than, not enough, insufficient, but if you need good, I want you to pray with me.

"Father, You are a good Father, who will not rob His children of good gifts. You said, no good thing will You keep from us. You are here, You gave to us, You will be with us even if we made our bed in hell. If we are in the highways or the byways, You are there also. You are as big and good as You say You are.

Help me, to redefine what is good. For some of us, what we say is good, is not good at all. For some of us what we want is not good, although we think it is our best. May You remind us that You gave us the good Gift of Your Son, to cover all the bad that we could ever do. The penalty for the bad, You have covered with the Good.

May You reach into our hearts today and restore order to what is good. May You give give me a heart to want good things. To pray good things. To meditate on good things night and day. You say to pray without ceasing, may I do that, and find the good.

May I not look at my poverty or lack, but look at all the good things You have put in my life on this day. Father, we thank You for being so good, better than we deserve, more than we ever expected. You are the hope of the world. You are love, You are good, You are wonderful, and so worthy to be praised. May this fruit of my lips continue to shape my heart to be grateful for all the good.

For those of us struggling, losing homes, marriages, children, death, despair, those who feel like they want to quit, Father, thank You for the good. Thank You for good music, thank You for hope. Thank You for the Good News. Thank You for the Gospel. Thank You for the Bible that is the foundation of our faith.

When we think the bad has overtaken us, thank You, Father, that You will stand in the gap for us. That You will raise a standard in us as the enemy attempts to come in like a rushing wind or crushing wave. May we not die under the direst we feel, the pressure, or what looks to be for our bad. Father, You said, You will turn everything to my good. No matter if it was intended for my good or my bad.

You say those who love You and are called according to Your purpose, You will bless, as to turn all things to our good. We thank You, we trust You, and we surrender our hope in this prayer under the authority of Christ Yashua (Jesus), amen."

# JOURNAL

## Share Your Thoughts or Answered Prayers

_____

_____

_____

_____

_____

_____

_____

_____

_____

_____

_____

_____

_____

_____

_____

_____

_____

_____

_____

_____

# PRAYER VESSEL

We are all a vessel, the Bible says. We are called to carry out our purpose and edify someone or something. I want to encourage you to consider what you are bringing to the world and how you are using your vessel.

"Oh Heavenly Father, thank You for giving us breath that fills our lungs. Before we were formed, You knew us and appointed us for a time such as this. You brought us here for a purpose, and Lord, we ask You to help us to remember that. We are more than how we feel at times or what we are told.

Father, You said that there are vessels of honor, dishonor, and common use. Help us today to be a battle ax in Your hands. Help us to be Your heart here on earth, sharing the good News of the Gospel! Help us to share compassion and understanding, to be patient, kind, and long-suffering if necessary. Not so we may boast, but so we can bring honor and glory to Your Name. We are to be a living sacrifice, which Paul says is our reasonable service.

Help us, Father, to give what we can and make no apologies for what we are not at the moment. We are more than conquerors through Christ, but we must be a vessel set apart for Your use. If we are distracted or acting contrary to Your plan, Father, open our eyes and hearts to follow You and not leave the road You already paved for us. Show us that better it is to live and love You by being obedient than leaning on our own understanding.

Father, You are all-knowing, and You can see what we cannot, and I thank You, Father, for not giving up on me when I thought to quit on myself. Showing me that I am more than I could ever imagine or see at times. Thank You for holding me up when I thought to give up. You have my heart and captured my soul. My Mighty Redeemer, thank You for changing the course of my life and giving me hope that I can be more than I am and was told I would be.

I want to be a vessel of honor, and if I bring You dishonor, correct that in me. Give me a new thirst for what is right and not what comes easy—if that is against Your plans for my life. Help me to be a vessel that demonstrates the time and love You put into me. It's so much I want to say, and so much I want to be. Help me to forgive myself when I am not perfect, and still see the love You have for me even in my imperfection.

It is in the name of Yahshua, that I say hallelujah and so be it!"

# JOURNAL

## Share Your Thoughts or Answered Prayers

_____

_____

_____

_____

_____

_____

_____

_____

_____

_____

_____

_____

_____

_____

_____

_____

_____

_____

PRAYER BELIEVER

If you have ever wondered if being a believer is the same as having a religious affiliation, I want to help guide you. The Bible was written to give us instructions, examples, hope, encouragement, and wisdom. The Word is an example of Yah's, God Almighty's Character, but it is not an exhaustive list of all He is, has done, could do, or will do. Join me in prayer for a greater understanding of what a believer is.

"Great Father, we thank You today for slowing us down to acknowledge You today. You are the King of Kings and the Lord of Lords. You are the only True God, greater than all other gods, and things we worship like gods. Thank You for being higher than us today so that we have a mighty Source to turn to for direction and comfort.

Father, it is written in the Bible to follow to the letter kills, but to live by the Spirit and be led by the Spirit gives life. Help us today to understand this mystery that shows us it is not about getting all the right answers that justify us, but us having Your Spirit and seal that claims us as Your child. We can make mistakes, and we will, but that doesn't boot us out of Your arms. You are faithful to us even when we are not to You or what You called us to do.

You show us that we are to be examples sent to the highways and byways to demonstrate to the world that You are a loving Father and Redeemer, sent to set the captives free! Father, thank You that vain religion or empty worship and praise is not what You want. You want a people who are affectionately known as Your children.

You have made room to make us joint heirs with Christ, because we need His blood to cover our sins. You have taken and made an act of love to cover us, which is deeper than any vain religious rite or ceremony. This is an act of love and one that atoned for our sins.

Father, we were living according to our own way. We were trying to do right, or willfully doing wrong. You have made us a believer that this way is not the design. You have shown us through the life of Christ how to live this life and how to follow Your Word even unto death. How to believe with all of our heart and trust the Word over everything we hear or feel.

Thank You, Father, for providing direction. Father, may You encourage those who think going to church or doing things to the letter is what You want, when what You desire is for them to love You, to see an do it. To love means spending time. Soften our hearts, teach us to be patient, and to understand. It is not about rushing through a Bible test, but about opening our hearts, minds, wills, and emotions to be led by You, Father.

Help us to slow down so that we see and give our lives to You. Being a believer is experiencing You, Father. For those who have never tasted You to know that You are good, help them to see You today. Reveal what they are missing and not seeing.

You are all around us, but are we sensitive enough to see You. As big, wonderful, and majestic as You are, it is a mystery how we could ever miss You—but we do! Help us, so that vain religion doesn't blind us or rob us of a healthy relationship with You. Show us how big and mighty You are to save! You are more than a religion, but You are the WAY, the TRUTH, and the LIFE. No one will enter into paradise without You. Father, guide us from here to where we are to spend eternity, in Jesus name, Amen."

# JOURNAL

## Share Your Thoughts or Answered Prayers

_____

_____

_____

_____

_____

_____

_____

_____

_____

_____

_____

_____

_____

_____

_____

_____

_____

_____

_____

_____

_____

## PRAYER EMPTY

If you feel empty today, good news, you don't have to stay this way. The good news is there is a world of wonderful things that the Father put here for you to endure any test. Let me encourage you!

"Father, our great Father, Ruler, and Protector. Thank You for being high and looking low today. Thank You for having a plan and a vision for our lives. Thank You that in our weakness, You are made strong. Thank You, Father, that we don't have to be superheroes to be loved by You.

We can be weak, we can be damaged, broken, even empty, and You take great joy in filling us up again. Thank You, Father, for never leaving nor forsaking us, but being right here with us. You are here holding our hands even when we don't feel You or see You. Thank You for being here for me in the late midnight hour, for wanting to bring me peace, and for helping me to endure what I thought I could not. For some of us who feel like we are on edge, thank You, Father, for recovering our souls right now in this moment by the authority of Christ Yahshua.

You said, those who are heavy laden, who have burdens, to come to You and You will give us rest. Thank You, Father, for being our resting place right now. Thank You, Father, for stabilizing the ground under our feet. For the many who feel broken, shattered, lonely, abandoned, and unloved, thank You for grasping our hand right now. Thank You for reaching into our lives and touching our souls and spirits.

Thank You for not giving up on us when we thought we were done. Thank You for not giving up on humanity when gross darkness seems to keep flooding the earth. Thank You for not giving up on us when we think to return to our past, our vomit, things that didn't work–thank You for turning our minds today. For turning our cravings and desires to sin against You, to sin no more.

For those of us who have failed and know it, Father lift us up today with this prayer. Remind us of who we are in You. Help us to forget what we heard, believed, yesterday if it is contrary to where we are in this moment. Help us to shield ourselves from the things that cause us to give up. That makes us say it is over when it is only for a night and not our whole lives.

Father, show us the way out. Give us the great escape! Show us how to make it out of here to get to where You want us to to be. Father, don't allow us to fail You today in our thoughts or how we treat others. Teach us how to be a respecter of who You are and who You called us to be. Teach us that we have value even when we think we don't.

Help us not to touch and agree with the enemy concerning how we see ourselves and our future. Father, bring us higher and help us to aspire to the plans You have for us. We thank You, Father, for showing us who we are in You. We are more than conquerors. We may feel that we have nothing left, but if we have You, it is more than enough!

You are more than enough to pull me out of this empty hole. I choose to believe that You are stronger than my problems. Bigger than my concerns. Bolder than whatever attempts to intimidate me. Regardless of what it is and could be, sickness, disease, heartbreak, disappointment, frustration, or anything else. You are Bigger Father, and I am stronger.

I will allow You to fill me with hope, joy, love, and direction. We will not fail, but shall overcome any test in the mighty name of Yahshua!"

## Share Your Thoughts or Answered Prayers

_____

_____

_____

_____

_____

_____

_____

_____

_____

_____

_____

_____

_____

_____

_____

_____

_____

_____

_____

_____

# PRAYER VICTORY

If you are feeling defeated, it is normal—but should not remain. If you are the child of the Most High God, good news! You will win! Let's pray for your victory.

"Father, You are a great God who will not fail us. You are bigger than our problems and more powerful than our worst enemies. You said that You will fight our battles and be our stronger tower. Father, we need You today.

Today, Your children are seeking Victory in our situation. Father, You have the glory, because without You, it will not be done. Father, guide us on the right path so that we can achieve the success—the victory You have for us in life. Show us the path we must follow to have great success, not just sometimes, but all the time.

Even when we look like we are failing, remind us that we are winners. We are powerful. We are loved. We are protected. Father, Thank You for reminding us today that we are winners.

If we fail when we try, we know this is only the learning curve and not the conclusion of the matter. What is impossible with man is possible with God. If we have made the grave mistake of not keeping You in our plans, forgive us now, Father.

Correct our mistake and show us a way out of this mistake. Teach us how to lean on You and not our own understanding. Thank You Father, that we are not losers. That we can block out the words of the enemy when he says that to us through anyone. We are a work in progress, and we thank You for reminding us that we can learn, make mistakes, and grow in Your hands.

You are not waiting to beat us for every mistake, but You are here patiently teaching us how to win and have victory! Today, I am encouraged because I know that I am made for my situation, so I won't worry. I won't doubt. I won't cry longer than I have to.

I am encouraged. I have hope. I know that I am loved and called for a time and purpose such as this. I will achieve what You sent me here to do in Yahshua's name, amen."

## Share Your Thoughts or Answered Prayers

_____

_____

_____

_____

_____

_____

_____

_____

_____

_____

_____

_____

_____

_____

_____

_____

_____

_____

_____

_____

# A Call to PRAY
K. Lee
30 day Experience Vol. 1 - 12

## Thank You!

PRAYER JOURNAL

If you haven't purchased a book from the series, please consider buying one copy and get access to all 12 digital copies as soon as they release! Get all 12 books, and get the audiobooks and digital books free!

Visit or Scan: AuthorKLee.com

For every 250 copies sold, we can publish the next book in the series. My goal is to publish all 12 within a calendar year and translate the book into 5 languages by year two. Purchase your book today, or download the free digital copies to support this series and share, please!

# FREE DOWNLOADS OR ORDER BOOKS

# PRAYER CONTENTMENT

In the Bible, Paul says how he had to learn to be content in all things. When he had a lot or a little. I want to encourage you today, if you are struggling with contentment, how to see your way through it.

"Father, oh great Father who knows Your plans for me and all of us! Thank You for being here and being the loudest Voice in my ears and heart. Remind me, Father, what it means to be a daughter or a son of Zion. A child of the Most High!

Thank You for being more than a friend or a God who judges me, but one who loves and is concerned about me! Father, You told us to be content in all things, trusting Your plans and Hand in our lives. Help us now to understand and be patient with what You see as the way forward. Help us to find joy in our advancement and success. Teach us to enjoy the good in our lives and not expect the bad.

Teach us that good things come to those who love You and are called to serve You. There are signs, miracles, and wonders that follow us as You promise. We thank You now, Father, for that. We also must thank You for the test that comes, too. We thank You for searching us to see what we can and cannot bear.

We thank You for giving us a way of escape through any trouble. We thank You that although some tests can become uncomfortable and less than ideal, we can lean on You. You are big enough and strong enough to carry me and see me through! Father, may You hold my hand and teach me how to move and keep my being. Teach me not to complain, but find the good.

Teach me to give You the glory for every situation, no matter what someone tries to do. No matter what the enemy's plans were, I am determined to give You praise from my lips. I will celebrate the good that gives me hope to change my circumstances if they are not bad. I will pray for a way of escape, and to endure if I must, but I will not complain and grow bitter with my circumstances.

Father, for those who have turned their joy to sorrow, may You remind them now that they are loved and You have plans for them that will come to pass. You have not forgotten about them nor their sacrifice. You said You will reward us in this life and the one to come.

Father, thank You for not being a liar but being able and willing to accomplish all that You set out to do in our lives. We celebrate You and will lift Your name High, Hosanna to the Highest, Father. You're a great God and a great Father.

Father, thank You for all we know and all we will learn as we trust You. In the precious name of Yahshua, hallelujah, so be it."

# JOURNAL

## Share Your Thoughts or Answered Prayers

_____

_____

_____

_____

_____

_____

_____

_____

_____

_____

_____

_____

_____

_____

_____

_____

_____

_____

_____

_____

## PRAYER RESPECT

If you are struggling to receive respect or to give it, that is a needed prayer. It is not the Father's will for you to tarry in this life, constantly being disrespected, though at times we must endure it. Respect is earned, but for some of us, that day will never come with certain people. I want to encourage you today. Let's pray.

"Father, our Respected Father, God, Creator, and all-powerful Being. We thank You today for sitting high and looking low. For being the One who set the world into motion and was mindful of each of us. Father, we thank You for Your goodness and love. We thank You for not leaving nor forsaking us.

We thank You for being the King of our lives and the ruler of our souls. As we learn to navigate this life, we thank You for not giving up on us and being our constant Guide. Father, we are coming to You because some of us are struggling to have the respect we deserve.

We are doing right by others, and they are abusing their influence in our lives. They are treating us with a lack of regard, and it is hurting our spirit. It is causing us harm, and we want to bring healing to this area. It is not Your will that we beg people to respect us.

You said that You will make our enemies our footstool. That You will cause those who don't regard us to respect us–even if that is the Yah in us they see. Help us, Father, to be patient with Your process in their lives. Help us not to grow anxious in well-doing but to be patient as we wait upon You to vindicate our names.

For those on the job dealing with disrespect, may You encourage them not to walk off prematurely. May we not get distracted by the enemy's tactics and end our journey prematurely. May we focus on what is the most important and not get distracted by what screams in our face disrespect.

Father, for those of us who are not receiving respect from our family members, may You change that around. May You remind us that You are the king, the one who sets plans in motion and establishes what is right or wrong. Father, if I am guilty of withholding respect where it is due, help me not to rob others of their due respect. Help me not to rob You, Father, of what belongs to You!

You are a good Father who deserves my best. If I am guilty of not giving it to You, turn my heart now, Father. Give me the eyes to see myself and not just everyone else' flaws. Show me how to decrease, how to be humble where I am prideful so that I can see the good in others.

We all have gifts. Help me to remember that when I think to compare and judge with hyper-criticism. Help me to remember to slow down and to show compassion. More can be done with honey than with vinegar. Give me the ability to be a peacemaker because You say, "Blessed is the peacemaker."

Count me amongst the blessed, Father. Teach me to respect those I should. Teach me to respect their office if I cannot respect them as individuals. Teach me to hold my tongue if that is necessary. Teach me to hold the line and to keep going even if others give up. Help me to stay the course. Keep me affixed and firm in serving the purpose You birthed me for in Jesus name.

# JOURNAL

## Share Your Thoughts or Answered Prayers

_____

_____

_____

_____

_____

_____

_____

_____

_____

_____

_____

_____

_____

_____

_____

_____

_____

_____

_____

_____

## PRAYER MISSION

Sometimes we can feel like we are aimlessly living life with no clear direction. We can feel that we were put on earth by accident, and there was no mission in sight. I want to remind you today that you have a purpose and a reason for being on earth. Let's go to God and seek it out.

"Father, You knew me before the foundation of the world. You knew me before my mom, dad, sister, or brother. You loved me before the foundation of the world, and in You, I have always existed. This world makes a great point of reinforcing how small we are and how seemingly insignificant we can be.

By intention, or accident, we can feel small and think that what we are and who we are is not enough. That we are just a number and not an important or vital piece in the world. Father, remind those who feel low today, who feel like they are just existing and barely hanging on, to know that You have plans for them. That each of us are numbered in Your sight, and You know us intimately. You know how many hairs are on our heads.

You know and hold every tear we have ever cried. You show us every day that we matter to You because You give us mercies new every day. You wake us up, and we live not on bread alone, but from every Word You speak concerning us. Thank You, Father, for speaking over my life and those in this prayer. Thank You for covering the world. Thank You for holding everything in it in place.

Thank You for showing us how to love You and be consistent. Father, for the mission that we can grow distant from, may You remind us that we have a purpose. A calling and a reason for why we are here on earth. We are not an accident, but an intentional force, a person with a mission sent to earth to bring our gifts and talents. If we ever think that we are nothing, thank You for reminding us that we are part of Your design for life.

We are in the world, but we are not solely of it. We have a mission set before us from heaven, and we desire not to miss it. Father, and great Redeemer, thank You for not leaving us hopeless. For showing us we have a mission, but also power to accomplish it. We have gifts and talents that the world needs.

No matter how small they may appear, in Your Hands, they can make a difference. Teach us our gifts and talents and how to regard them. How to put them in the best environment to achieve what You have birthed us for. Some of us are sent to help children, others adults, others, women or men. Teach us where we belong. Some bless animals or plants.

Then others, buildings, streets, technology, or food. We can be gifted in many ways, but our mission is to give You glory and achieve our purpose for which You sent us to earth. There is nothing too small. We learn by the hearing of each other's testimonies, so even hearing each other's success stories or failures, we can bless those around us. Bless us to remove the shame we have about what we have done and not done.

Remind us of what is important and what is a trap from the enemy to keep us discouraged or distracted. We are glad we don't have to work our mission alone, but we can stand together, and for those who believe, with the Body of Christ also, to achieve our mission in life. In the precious name of Jesus, Yahshua the Prince of Peace, we say hallelujah and it is done!"

# JOURNAL

## Share Your Thoughts or Answered Prayers

_____

_____

_____

_____

_____

_____

_____

_____

_____

_____

_____

_____

_____

_____

_____

_____

_____

_____

_____

# PRAYER PURPOSE

If you have been chasing your purpose or wondering if there is a purpose to life, I want to encourage you today. There is a reason for you being here on earth. Your purpose is not floating outside of you, but was born within you. Let's pray for your purpose.

"Father, great and knowledgeable God, we thank You for Your goodness. We thank You for being holy and teaching us how to be more like You. We thank You for showing us the mercy we need and giving us hope when times can be discouraging. Father, as we look at Your Great works, we fall into awe. You are good, wonderful, kind, loving, and powerful.

Father, I am coming to You today because I am in search of my purpose. I know I am talented and I believe those talents have a place on earth. But if I am honest, I am struggling to connect the dots between my talents and my purpose. I am coming to You, Father, to ask that You direct my heart and plans.

I feel like like I am going in circles. I take steps ahead then steps behind. I feel like I am doing good, but unsure of how much I am pleasing You. I don't want to live this life doing everything, thinking I am working to please You, only to find that I was far away too much of my life. I am feeling drained, and I want to be filled back up.

I know the word and parts of my story, but I need You to open my heart and eyes again to see what I don't see right now. I need to feel what I am not feeling. Connect me back to my purpose and the source for why I was brought to earth. I know greater works I am able to do because of what You have done through the Messiah. But I am uncertain of how I fit into this glorious picture that I desperately want to find a place in.

Show me how to enter the Kingdom of God. Show me my gifts and talents and how to weave them into the Kingdom assignment I was born to accomplish. I know living and making money is a part of life, but I also know it is not all that life is. I need You, Father, to touch me again. To remind me of how wonderful You are.

I need You to reach me in my secret place, and if I am in a dark place, to pull me out. Father, lift me out of this space so that I might glorify You and bring glory to Your name. Deliver me from this feeling of inadequacy. Show me how to walk in my purpose. Show me how to take back my life.

Remind me of its value if I have forgotten. If I am unfocused, distracted from my path, give me tunnel vision long enough to make it out of the darkness into the light. Father, accelerate me forward so that I can please You now, in Yahshua's name. Father set me free in mind and spirit so that I will not stay in this same place another day or for another season. Deliver me, Father.

And I ask, Father, for You to Fill me up now and endow me with power to change my life from the inside out. Give me strength and confidence not to quit in well-doing. I know I am not a mistake. I know I have a purpose. I know I was brought to earth for a reason, and if I am a new creature in Christ, a believer, walking by the Spirit, I am called to give You glory. Father, bless my actions and words to bless You, in Yahshua's name, amen."

# JOURNAL

## Share Your Thoughts or Answered Prayers

_____

_____

_____

_____

_____

_____

_____

_____

_____

_____

_____

_____

_____

_____

_____

_____

_____

_____

_____

_____

# PRAYER PATTERNS

If you have recognized concerning patterns in your life, that is a good sign. You will not pray about anything you are not aware exists. If you are at a point where you can pray about what you do on autopilot, you are ready to seek the Father and make the changes necessary.

"Father, oh great God of decency and order. We thank You for being here and everywhere all at one time. We thank You for being a loving Father who loves us and has called us for Your purpose. Father, please put an end to the patterns that I do that go against You. The sins I create, or the choices I make that mean me no good.

Help me to stop being my worst enemy or allowing toxic patterns to repeat in my mind, heart, or actions. Show me the error of my ways and the root of my patterns. Father, You say whatever we bind on earth is bound in heaven, whatever we loose on earth is loosed in heaven.

Father, now we loose the power to expose our shortcomings. We loose the maturity to handle our true reality. We loose the ability to hear what You say concerning what we see. We shut the mouths of the enemy so we may hear You clearly. So that we can build our confidence as we face giants. Old truths, old lies, and anything in between.

Thank You Father, for being bigger than our challenges. When we were young, we weren't strong enough to battle disappointment. We are today through Your strength! We thought we were weak, but Father, You say in You we are more than conquerors. Thank You for being our strength today. Thank You for exposing the enemy today for our progress. Thank You for breaking chains and leaving them disconnected.

Thank You for giving us the power to face our truth, the truth. Father, help us to love being free more than bondage. Teach us to be on one accord with You. Let us not fight against You to protect patterns that harm us, help us not to hide behind shame, blame, fear, or guilt. Remind us that You have set us free and You are the answer to all things.

Thank You for loving me today and showing me out of the wilderness of habitual patterns. Teach me how to be set free from ideas, thoughts, patterns that I could not break without You. Thank You for being a chain breaker, miracle worker, and healer. Thank You for healing my heart, mind, soul, and emotions. Keep me, Father, as I battle myself and the lies I have believed.

Remind me, oh God, I am stronger today than I was yesterday, moments ago, yester-years. I am here, and I am not alone! Thank You for being here with me, Father, for never leaving me nor forsaking me. Bless Your mighty name, Oh God."

# JOURNAL

## Share Your Thoughts or Answered Prayers

_____

_____

_____

_____

_____

_____

_____

_____

_____

_____

_____

_____

_____

_____

_____

_____

_____

_____

_____

_____

## PRAYER
## FAMILIAR SPIRITS

If you are finding that your life is not only going in a circle, but it seems like the same spirit keeps coming back. It can be a different person, but they do the same actions and treat you the same way. They can have similar character traits or say similar words that trigger something deep in your spirit. If so, let's pray against familiar spirits.

"Father, we thank You for being all in all. We thank You for being all-powerful, and we thank You for revealing the enemy that accuses us and pursues us day and night. We thank You, Father, that You have not left us lost on how the enemy works. You said that when a spirit dwells with us, when he is cast out, if we are not filled by You, they will come back with more to reclaim the one lost. Father, if we have given our lives to You but withheld ourselves from being filled by You, forgive us now.

Forgive us for lying to ourselves but also

for lying to You. For saying we will when we had no intention. Father, forgive us for calling on Your name to ask for Your gifts but disowning Your spirit and displacing You outside of our hearts, minds, and bodies. Father, we know now that we need You.

We know that we need You to enter our lives and take over every inch of space we know or could imagine we have. Father, we need to be filled by You because we are seeing familiar spirits, problems, and mistakes that captured our family are now trying to capture us. Things we did in our youth are now back and tempting us. We know that if we do not have You, we will fall into the same lust, same problems, same sins, and agree with old familiar spirits.

Father, deliver me if I have slipped, and now I am seeing it. Forgive me, Father, for taking my eyes off of You for even a moment, and I was overtaking. Father, redeem me again. Fill me again. Show me if I have forgotten why I needed You, my Lord and Savior. Father, I thank You now for reaching into my life and giving me the strength to rebuke and reject familiar spirits.

For those struggling with drinking, Father, remind them why they sought Your Face to begin with. Father, for those struggling with emotional well-being, heal them, God. For those struggling with language, heal their lips. For those battling negative thoughts, heal their minds, oh God. For those who are out of balance now, Father bless them to achieve a life balance You design.

Thank You for Your patience and how You can take us into Your bosom even when we are at fault. Thank You, Father, that You are our strong Tower we can run to in our times of need. Teach us how to discern spirits and know who is behind the face, the action, the words we hear. Teach us how to fight in the spirit, spiritual problems. As we face old demons, empower us to overcome them and kick them out for good.

Give us Your Word and truth—give us the power to resist the devil and his teachings. Father, we thank You, oh God, for how good You have been to us. We thank You for Your shelter and forgiveness. In Yahshua's name, amen."

# JOURNAL

## Share Your Thoughts or Answered Prayers

_____

_____

_____

_____

_____

_____

_____

_____

_____

_____

_____

_____

_____

_____

_____

_____

_____

_____

_____

_____

# PRAYER MISTAKES

We are all going to make mistakes. There are no perfect people, but we all stand in the need of God's heavenly hand. We all need Him to deliver us and cover us through our mistakes. If you are struggling with mistakes you made or someone else, I want to encourage you.

"Father, You are a perfect God who has a perfect plan for our lives. Thank You for being so kind and willing to love Your creation. Thank You for sending Your Son to redeem us as the Second Adam. Father, we wanted to come to You in prayer because we have made mistakes, and we are living with the mistakes of others. Help us, Father, to see the good and the lessons that can be learned from our mistakes.

Teach us how to make our lives better and not worse. Teach us how to turn around what looks like a losing battle for a win. Teach me how to forgive myself. I know sometimes when terrible things happen and we feel we are the blame—or we are at fault, it is hard to move on.

It is hard to unsee what we have seen or done. Give us the power to forgive ourselves and others. Show us how to bring You honor and not disgrace. Help me to rebuild anything that I have broken and recover anything that I have lost.

Thank You, Father, for being my rock and Redeemer. In Yahshua's name, amen."

## Share Your Thoughts or Answered Prayers

_____

_____

_____

_____

_____

_____

_____

_____

_____

_____

_____

_____

_____

_____

_____

_____

_____

_____

_____

# A Call to PRAY
K. Lee

day Experience
Vol. 1 - 12

## Thank You!

PRAYER JOURNAL

If you haven't purchased a book from the series, please consider buying one copy and get access to all 12 digital copies as soon as they release! Get all 12 books, and get the audiobooks and digital books free!

Visit or Scan: AuthorKLee.com

For every 250 copies sold, we can publish the next book in the series. My goal is to publish all 12 within a calendar year and translate the book into 5 languages by year two. Purchase your book today, or download the free digital copies to support this series and share, please!

## FREE DOWNLOADS OR ORDER BOOKS

# PRAYER LESSONS

If you are living, you are going to face challenges. There are lessons we cannot run from and must face. If you are at a point in your life where you need to learn or teach lessons, join me in this prayer.

"Father, our great Father and protector, thank You for being the leader of my soul and my redeemer. You are good and so worthy to be praised. Father, I know in this life there are lessons we must learn. We might think to avoid the lessons because they hurt, bring us shame or blame, but Father help us to finish the lessons You start in us.

Build up our confidence and help us to endure the challenges that come with working to pass a test. We know that some tests come to the strong and at times when we feel the least prepared. May we lean on You when we feel powerless to fight. You say in our weakness, You are made strong.

Father, help me to remember the point of a test. It is not to beat me down or to oppress me, but to teach me a lesson that I will pass with Your help and guidance. Father, if I am repeating a lesson because I have failed it before, help me not to get discouraged. Silence the enemy's voice in my ears, my doubts, or fears about passing a lesson.

Help me to realize not everyone in my life is meant to stay forever; some are for a lesson. Help me not to hate people because they brought a lesson. Teach me how to appreciate the tests and lessons in my life because this is how I mature. Remind me today, Father, of what is most important.

May I not only take this lesson, but also help me to master what I am afraid of. Give me boldness, confidence, and strength to endure lessons–and be teachable. In Jesus name, amen."

## Share Your Thoughts or Answered Prayers

_____

_____

_____

_____

_____

_____

_____

_____

_____

_____

_____

_____

_____

_____

_____

_____

_____

_____

# PRAYER STINGY

If you have a problem sharing what you have with others. You should ask why this is so difficult for you. Is this a pattern or a mindset? Are you greedy, or just feel like there is not enough? The Father blesses a cheerful giver, so if you are missing out on this blessing, let's go to Yah in prayer.

"Father, You are the good God who gives and takes away. Father, You have given us the best example to show us why we should give and be givers, but I am struggling today to give to someone I love. You said blessed are those who will give, and giving is better than receiving.

Father, there are many who struggle to give anything to someone else, sometimes giving someone what they deserve is even a task. Father, expand my mind and heart to appreciate and trust You more with my resources. Help me not to worry about the things that keep me awake at night and block my desire to give.

Being stingy doesn't leave me with more, but robs me of the gift to receive where I have sown. Show me the hurtful action of stinginess and remind me why I shouldn't do it. For those who will eat up everything from someone else, and then when they need, they won't help them, show them that this is wrong.

This is like stealing, and Yah, You are not a thief, and Your children should not be either. Increase my heart to share and to be fair. Help me to stop being so selfish, where the only person I care about is me, and remind me that we live on earth in a community.

We are to share resources. For those who are married, if one partner is not willing to share and complains when they must, reveal this hurtful pattern to them. Show them that no one person is better than the whole. We are interconnected, and we need each other. Remind us that holding out on people is not how You get ahead in relationships.

There are times when we should use wisdom for what we share about ourselves, but we should never manipulate or lie by omission. Father, You said to resist the devil, to bind this spirit of stealing and lying, so the devil will leave. Show us how we are lying to others, ourselves, and stealing.

Keep us from being thieves and liars. Deliver us from ourselves in Jesus name. Amen!"

# JOURNAL

## Share Your Thoughts or Answered Prayers

_____

_____

_____

_____

_____

_____

_____

_____

_____

_____

_____

_____

_____

_____

_____

_____

_____

_____

_____

_____

# PRAYER GIVING

The gift of giving is a gift that keeps on giving. If you are a giver, I pray that the Father will fill you back up again. Givers are needed in this world because they spread the wealth. If you are a giver or want to be, join me in prayer.

"Father, and Great I Am, thank You for being present in my life and the world. Thank You for never leaving nor forsaking me. Thank You for calling me a son or daughter of Yours, making me a child when I could have been Your enemy at times in my life.

Oh, gracious Father, my Rock and Savior, thank You for giving Your Son on Calvary so that we may be free and live more abundantly. Father, I thank You for giving me a heart to give to others. Thank You for instilling this desire in my heart and others. The world needs givers and more of them still.

You say the greatest among men and women are those who serve, those who are willing to give to others. Help us today, Father, to give more. To give when we can, when we think we can't, if You said yes, because we trust Your Hand. Give us the ability to give You thanks for the good and bad times.

Gift us with hope, and to know smiling and making a joyful noise is a gift that keeps on giving. Show us how to give back to You because You have done and continue to do so much for us. Stop us from giving for people to like us, but to give out of service and gratitude to You. Help us to give what we can, but not overextend ourselves. Teach us wisdom in finances so that we can manage what we have. Help us to realize our giving is not saving people; it is a blessing to people.

We are not anyone's Source, but You are! Show us to point others to a giving relationship with You so that they, too, can become givers with the right heart. For those who struggle to give, show them how giving benefits everybody. Remind them that they, too, are the benefactor of giving. They too can be the ones to bless others and not always need a blessing.

It feels good to receive, but even better to give! Remind us to give back to You, Father, those we love, to the poor who You say will be with us always. It is what we do for those who cannot pay us back that You reward us for. You said You would be indebted to no man, so thank You for giving to us in this life and the one to come. In the precious name of Yahshua, we say hallelujah and so be it!"

# JOURNAL

## Share Your Thoughts or Answered Prayers

_____

_____

_____

_____

_____

_____

_____

_____

_____

_____

_____

_____

_____

_____

_____

_____

_____

_____

_____

_____

_____

# PRAYER GIFTS

Gifts are a joy to have. They are reminders of someone's love or commitment, and they can bring comfort to us in our times of need. They are also celebrations of something great we have done or a milestone we have achieved.

"Father, You are our greatest gift and champion to all humankind. Thank You for being on my side. Thank You for fighting the battles I could not and cannot fight. Thank You for giving me the gift of peace today. Thank You for keeping my mindset on You and the good things You do.

Father, show me how to love You and give You more of me because You have already given me everything I need. I offer up my self to You because it is the greatest gift I have. Father, thank You for making me valuable—even priceless by breathing Your Spirit into my lungs. Thank You for the gift of life and, further, for Your Son who gives us the abundant life. Thank You for not counting my wrongs but being willing to give me gifts while I learn, and when I wasn't trying.

The gift of mercy is one I cannot give enough thanks for. Father, shower us with Your mercy, forgiveness, wisdom, and truth. The gifts You give go way beyond money and things, and these are the things I appreciate. Thank You for meeting my needs today. Thank You for caring about me. Father, thank You for helping me to see gifts as a form of love.

No, gifts of things are not everything, but gifts given out of love mean everything. For those who struggle to accept gifts, help to guide their hearts. Show them that receiving and giving gifts are both necessary. You are someone who needs to know that you are loved. We all need to feel loved and appreciated, and this is why we move like how we do.

I want to encourage anyone who feels like they don't deserve a gift to know that it is okay if you did not deserve the gift given to you. This is what makes gifts even sweeter. We cannot control who gives to us, but we can control is how we respond. We can show our gratitude and thanks. For those who are trying to show their gratitude for what others have done for them, words can be used, actions, and responding positively to the gift.

Help us all, Father, to show our gratitude for what others have given and done for us. From the military to hospital staff, family members, and clergy, give is the power to say thank you. Sometimes it is just words of thanks, and other times, it is words of action. Thank You, Father, for guiding us to give and receive gifts. Thank you for the greatest gift, Your Son.

Thank You for Your redeeming power, love, and patience. When we think to deny a gift or to not give a gift, remind us that we are giving out of our abundance and not poverty, even if it looks like it. We have more than enough because everything will be added to us for those who seek and serve the Lord. Thank You for being a rewarded of those who diligently seek You, Father. In the name of Yahshua, amen."

# JOURNAL

## Share Your Thoughts or
## Answered Prayers

_____

_____

_____

_____

_____

_____

_____

_____

_____

_____

_____

_____

_____

_____

_____

_____

_____

_____

_____

# PRAYER ABUNDANCE

Having more than enough is what abundance is. Walking in the overflow is a place that exists, and if you have not been there or are striving to get there, be encouraged with this prayer.

"Father, our God of plenty and more than enough. Thank You that everything on earth belongs to You! We acknowledge that Your gifts and power are unmatched by anyone or anything anywhere and at anytime. You are the great God, the Great I Am. Thank You for making us, Your creation.

Thank You for giving us the power to serve You, the will, and the ability to know the way. Your Word is a lamp to our feet and a path that will lead us out of the wilderness. Thank You for the concept of abundance. In our lives, many of us can look around and see financial, social, emotional, or political strain. We can see the unrest and interact with it.

Father, we are asking You to change us. As You change us, we will impact the world. None of us are superheroes on our own, but for those of us in the Kingdom of God, we make up the Body of Christ. What is impossible with man is made possible through Christ, the Living Word, and we thank You, Father for that! You said through Christ, greater works are we able to do because our Lord and Savior sits at the right hand of the Father and intercedes for us.

Thank You, Father, that Your word is sustaining us now. That Your word is speaking life even if we thought to speak death concerning our lives. Father, the abundant life is where we need to be in mind, body, and spirit. Help us to uncover that today. Help us to understand what it means to be at peace in You. To know that all things are beneath Your feet.

Anything is possible for those who believe; increase our belief today. Remove the scales from our eyes, in Jesus name, so that we can see, believe, and have hope for more. For those who are too comfortable in their poverty and they prefer not enough over abundance, change this in us. Remind us, those who have forgiven much love much. They do a lot in hopes to show their gratitude, and that's great.

But Father, You are also a rewarder to those who diligently seek You. You will pour out blessings on our life we don't have room to receive. We need You now, Father, to eradicate lack in our lives. Touch our finances today, our hope, our dreams, our futures, families, businesses, and emotions.

Give us a good understanding for what the abundant life means and how we can show our gratitude. Teach us how to stay in the overflow. Teach us how to trust You when it is easy, and even if it gets scary.

Father, bind the spiritual and natural influences that attempt to block the plans You have for me. If my mouth is causing drought, correct my language. Rework my thoughts, and thank You for finishing a work You started in me, Father. In Yahshua's name, hallelujah and so be it!"

# JOURNAL

## Share Your Thoughts or Answered Prayers

_____

_____

_____

_____

_____

_____

_____

_____

_____

_____

_____

_____

_____

_____

_____

_____

_____

_____

_____

_____

_____

# PRAYER
# WORD

The Word who knew no sin became sin so that we can live again. So that we can have a chance at redemption—not that the blood wasn't enough, but that we could deny the power of it. For some of us, still, our own words don't mean much, so it is hard for us to grasp concepts that we could learn through Christ, the Living Word, becoming flesh. Today, I want us to pray about valuing our words, the words of others, but most importantly, the Word of God. Let us pray.

"Father, You are a good, good Father, and that is all You can be. You are loving, kind, patient, and full of mercy. You are good to us when we don't deserve it, and You share Your wisdom and love if only we could see and appreciate it. For some of us, we don't appreciate the Word of God, the Messiah, because we don't understand who He is. We don't understand what it means for Jesus, Yahshua in the

Hebrew, to set us free.

For Him to be the source for how we move, live, and have our being. Help us, Father, to understand this mystery and for it not to elude us. Father, Your Word is so powerful that everything that is, was brought into being through Christ Jesus. We are all here today and everything under the sun because You spoke it into existence. A glimpse of this power, You have given to humanity, in that we can speak life through the power of our words.

Teach us today that our words have power. They are not as powerful as Yours. We will never be stronger than our Creator—our Master, but we can strive to be more like You. Father, it is Your will that we all look like Your Word, Yahshua, our Lord and Savior. You are the example before the world, and You are the King Designer of all life.

You are full of power and majesty; we would be foolish not to stand in awe of You. Father, it is now that we ask for You to remind us of how powerful our words are. We may be used to people misunderstanding or having selective memory when it comes to us. Can you help us embrace our power and strength? Remind us that we are more than conquerors.

Stronger is He that is within us than anything in the world. Although we might struggle and look like we have lost a battle, we will win the war. Father, show up strong, mighty in battle concerning the situations I face. If I have spoken an idle word, or if You are using me to speak, and I am silent. Please forgive me, Father, and help reorder my words and my steps.

Help me to be a believer of Your Word. Help me to see the power in speaking. Teach me, Father, how to speak and do what I say. Break my apathy for words. Erase the pain and trauma associated with words that cause me to lose faith in You or in myself.

Restore the value I should have for Your words and my own. Help me to hold myself accountable and those who speak words to me. Words have power. Today, every word that was said that pulled my power or attempted to steal Your glory, I pull down from my mind and away from my heart. I will choose to believe Your Word over the words of others. I choose to believe The Truth over every lie or vain imagination that rises against You. In Yahshua's name, amen and hallelujah."

# JOURNAL

## Share Your Thoughts or Answered Prayers

_____

_____

_____

_____

_____

_____

_____

_____

_____

_____

_____

_____

_____

_____

_____

_____

_____

_____

_____

_____

# PRAYER ETERNAL LIFE

For some of us, eternal life seems like a dream. We are struggling with the here and now, or praying that a good day will come. For those who have lost loved ones, we believe we will see them again because our names are in the book of life. We pray and hope for eternal life in heaven, and not just to live eternally. Join me if you want your eternity to be spent in heaven or if you seek wisdom about eternity.

"Father, the eternal God, the keeper of life and my soul. Thank You for smiling on me today. Thank You, for never giving up on me, even when I thought to quit on myself. Father, hold my hand today and keep me part of Your masterful plan.

Father, You are the only one who could understand eternity. You are eternal, without beginning and end. You know how to exist and always remain, and always have been. Father, guide me today, and those who are seeking understanding about eternal life. Father, show us how to live this life and to go forth into this world without becoming of it.

Father, eternal is everlasting. Father, You said that those who are called to be with You in heaven will have eternal life. For those who accept the gift of salvation, they can taste death, but it will have no sting because we get to enter a rest with You. Father, to think of a life where it never ends and leaving here only begins the next phase of life can be scary and hard.

Father, for those of us who fear the unknown or eternity, show us that we don't have to fear. You are the keeper of our souls, and You know how to guide us through this time on earth and the one after. You are Spirit, and not flesh and bone. You are holy, and to spend eternity with You in a holy place, You require us to be born again by accepting Your Word as the foundation of our lives and Your Son as our Lord and Savior.

Help us to reduce in this life so that we have an eternity we can enjoy. No one wants to go to hell, although many feel they deserve it or someone else does. Thank You for mercy and grace to afford us a life we don't deserve, but we desperately need. We need to be set free and to know there is life after this.

For those barely holding on, hoping to die

here to go with you now, encourage them to be prepared to walk with You on earth as well as heaven. If their time is not up, remind them of their calling and power. Remind them that we won't miss a thing because You will never leave us nor forsake us, no matter the test.

Thank You for being an unmovable God. Thank You for being loving, kind, and patient. I trust You, Father, to show me how to ready myself for eternity. A place where time doesn't exist, it does not control or govern space or experience; only You do. Father, we trust You now to lead the way so that we can spend eternity with You and not separate from You, in Jesus' name, amen."

# JOURNAL

## Share Your Thoughts or
## Answered Prayers

---

---

---

---

---

---

---

---

---

---

---

---

---

---

---

---

---

---

---

---

---

---

# PRAYER DISOBEDIENT

If you are dealing with the fallout from disobedience, I want to encourage you. The seed of disobedience can run wild if it is not checked. If you have not recognized or called out the spirit of rebellion and disobedience in your life, your children, or surrounding you, let's do it now.

"Father, You are the God of decency and order. Father, You are a wise ruler and loving king. Lord, I am coming to You because someone I love is battling the spirit of rebellion and disobedience. Father, You tell us to obey our mother and father so that our days will be long. If we are being disobedient to the fathers and mothers You put in our lives to guide us, please forgive us.

Father, show us how we are being disobedient and not listening. If we are to follow Your voice and mute all others, Father, guide us in this way also. Teach us how to stand strong on truth and Your divine direction over what my sound good or looks good.

Encourage my faith in Your word and direction if my faith is too weak. Father, bind the enemy from speaking to me now so that I may hear Your voice and discern the direction You have for me. If there is a direction I should encourage my children, family, loved ones, or company, help me to hear Your voice over the noise.

Silence my inner thoughts or fears if they are leading me to be disobedient to Your instructions or guidance. Teach me to be sensitive to the right voices. Help me to have the strength to do what is right, even if I stand alone. It is better to stand alone on the truth You gave me than to stand with the crowd if that means being disobedient to Your instructions.

Help me to have tunnel vision to focus on Your instruction so that I may learn You even more. In the precious name of Yahshua, we say hallelujah and so be it."

## Share Your Thoughts or Answered Prayers

_____

_____

_____

_____

_____

_____

_____

_____

_____

_____

_____

_____

_____

_____

_____

_____

_____

_____

_____

_____

_____

# A Call to PRAY

K. Lee

30 day Experience Vol. 1 - 12

PRAYER JOURNAL

## Thank You!

If you haven't purchased a book from the series, please consider buying one copy and get access to all 12 digital copies as soon as they release! Get all 12 books, and get the audiobooks and digital books free!

Visit or Scan: AuthorKLee.com

For every 250 copies sold, we can publish the next book in the series. My goal is to publish all 12 within a calendar year and translate the book into 5 languages by year two. urchase your book today, or download the free digital copies to support this series and share, please!

# PRAYER PLEASURE

People will tell us life is all about us and our pleasure. Pleasure is not a sin in the right context, but we can fall in love with pleasure and forget that the pleasure we want or desire should be authorized. This prayer is for healthy pleasure and the strength to change what is broken. Join me.

"Father, You know what pleasure feels like. I thank You for being a mighty God who is aware of His creation. You know me, although I am as small as an ant from heaven, if not a speckle of dust, yet You know my name and every hair on my head. Thank You for loving me and taking Your time to understand me, Your created.

There is nothing new under the sun, but You faithfully make each day new. Thank You for new mercies every day. Father, I know there are guilty pleasures I have that I need Your help to break. If I am displeasing You through what I crave or desire, reveal it to me.

Show me how I am offending You and missing the mark. Help me to pick the right person and be patient as I wait for authorized passion. Teach me that lust is fleeting and doesn't last. It might feel good, but this pleasure over time turns to sorrow.

Father, I don't want to hurt to have love in my life. I want to grow in love and share it with others. Thank You for Your direction and power to please You first. Search me, Father, and anything that displeases You about me, expose it in Jesus name.

Show me how I need to improve to make You happy and confirm what I desire. You said You will give us the desire of our hearts, Father, help me to desire more. Help me to believe for more and be a better steward over my life than I have been. Thank You for the family I have and the one You are building.

May we all find peace in You and hope to believe what is hard to conceive, eternal life, because You promised us we shall have it. How we spend our eternity is the best choice and freedom You could ever give to us. In the name of Yahshua, so be it."

## Share Your Thoughts or Answered Prayers

_____

_____

_____

_____

_____

_____

_____

_____

_____

_____

_____

_____

_____

_____

_____

_____

_____

_____

_____

_____

_____

*Pleasure*

## PRAYER EXPERIENCE

In life, we experience it, do we not? Life is a journey filled with situations, people, tasks, assignments, and etc. If you are new to the world, you likely have less experience than someone who is more mature.

There is good news for experience; there is nothing new under the sun. Age isn't everything. If your life experience is challenging, happy, or fun, we can pray about it.

"Father, You are the Creator of life and experience. The wise One, who knows what Your plans are and how Your plans have changed because of the choices of people or spiritual powers. Thank You for preparing a way for our escape, no matter the test or actions of others. Thank You for ensuring we have Your Word, and would not be blindsided by the enemy's plans.

You expose the liar, his plans, and agenda

in the Bible, but also through Your prophets. Thank You for the pastors, teachers, evangelists, and those with helps who are sent to earth to help Your children live out their experience. We thank You for mothers and fathers, siblings, uncles, grandparents, and mentors.

We need them to help us achieve what You set us out to do in this world. Remind us all to cherish the time we have because time runs in one timeline, straight. We don't get a redo or to go in reverse. Help us to remain focused in our youth, and as we grow older, so we live with very little regrets.

There will be mistakes in our life experience, but Father, thank You for turning them to our good. Thank You for showing us the way and how to move on. We need You, Father, no matter our age, to show us how to experience life. To be the one guiding us and walking with us. The one who brings us comfort and correction.

Father, thank You for being a good Father to those who allow You to be one for their lives and their families. Thank You for being a mentor and wise counsel for those who invite You into their businesses, their dreams, and plans. Father, You are all-knowing, but You still give us free choice. Thank You for the power we have and the wisdom You make available to yield it well.

Thank You for Your awesome plan for life and humanity, and Your forgiveness for how we messed that up in the beginning until now. Thank You for being an active Creator who is involved, approachable, hears us, and is mindful of us. Hold our hands now as we journey through life experiences and hard-felt emotions. Teach us to balance our thoughts and to trust You for all things. In the name of Jesus, amen."

# JOURNAL

## Share Your Thoughts or Answered Prayers

_____

_____

_____

_____

_____

_____

_____

_____

_____

_____

_____

_____

_____

_____

_____

_____

_____

_____

_____

# PRAYER MUSIC

Music is a joyful noise that brings us fun, experiences, and can turn the tide of our day. Sometimes we listen to music that can also do the opposite, bring the mood down, and have us self-reflect or experience regret. There is power in music, a message, and spirits. Consider the music you sing and listen to, and if you are not able to break the cycle and listen to something else without excuse, we must pray.

"Father, our God, full of wisdom and love, thank You for being in our midst. Thank You for hearing us today and being present for our questions and concerns. Thank You for being a Father who loves us and is concerned about us and our cares. Father, we thank You for creating music and all that it can do to show us more of You.

We know the enemy's job is to pervert the good and turn it for our bad. Father, music is one of those gifts given to Lucifer that when we lose sight of the one who gave music, we can allow the many who manipulate music to trick us into ideologies, emotions, and entertain spirits unaware. Father, You said to guard our minds, hearts, and ears because the enemy roams around like a roaring lion seeking to destroy.

Music is a wonderful gift, but we have to understand the spirit behind the song, behind the music. Help us to see what we don't see in the natural. Help us to be honest about what we see in the natural and not deny it, because we don't like it. Father, for some of us, we pick people to listen to that we know don't have a message of love, understanding, peace, joy, or godliness.

We say, I just like the beat, or we just like this or that but don't pay attention to the words or intent. Father, bind this lie, expose it so it has nowhere to run. We like the music and what we choose to watch, because something about it has captivated us. We are enticed by something or someone. We might not know the depths of our attraction, but something has gotten into us, and we struggle to let it out.

Father, help us to think on good things, things that are lovely, kind, are true, are honest, are just, are pure, are lovely, are of good report, if there be any virtue or if there be anything worth celebrating, think on these things. Father, help us to rid ourselves of music that is the opposite. Music that spews hatred, lies, defames, creates sexual perversion, and belittles the value of men, women, and children.

Help us to fall in love with love music and not sex songs. Help us to understand the things that are true from someone's life experience, then work to solve the problems and not glorify the enemy. Teach us how to interpret songs and pull down the demons and their practices hidden in music.

Father, we ask that You expose the lies shared in music. That You will raise up a beacon in us that will tell us not to listen to what You don't want us to anymore. That You will cause evil music that circles in our ears to bring us no joy. No fun. That we can hear the lyrics and choose not to sing it. That we can see the video or watch the movie, and it no longer thrills us.

Father, restructure our expectations and what we consider joyful and entertaining. Be on our hands as we turn the dial to tune into music. Show us how to be present and sense the spirit in the beat, not just in the lyric. Help us to feel and sense the heaviness in songs, so that we shut it off from impacting our spirit.

Show us the fault in our music selection and lead us to music that will lift us up. Keep us encouraged, teach us, and help us to enjoy moments in our lives and reflect. Teach us to love gospel music and songs that build us spiritually. Help us to find true love songs that will help us enjoy our spouse in a clean atmosphere.

Remove sexual perversion from our appetite in our music selection. Remove our thirst for violence in songs. Control our thoughts, Father, and deliver us from the snares sent into the world through music.

Bind the witches and warlocks on assignment to win the souls of the saved, to seduce us to live lifestyles contrary to our calling on earth. Break this yoke and the power of smoking, drugs, and alcohol that pairs too well with the music. Set the captives free now in Yahshua's name, so be it!"

## Share Your Thoughts or Answered Prayers

_____

_____

_____

_____

_____

_____

_____

_____

_____

_____

_____

_____

_____

_____

_____

_____

_____

_____

_____

# PRAYER UNSATISFIED

Things in our lives can leave us unsatisfied, can't it? We can think we are doing all of this to get something, and when it falls short of what we expected, we can feel unsatisfied. Unsatisfied with results, a situation, or someone's actions is all possible. If you feel unsatisfied with life, family, your job, or circumstances, I want you to join me in prayer.

"Father, thank You for being a rewarder of those who diligently seek You. Thank You for being the king of my life who knows the plans You have for me and all of us. Father, You say a workman is worthy of their hire.

If I work, I should be paid, but Father, I have been working, and the results are lackluster. They are not enough, and they have left me unsatisfied. I am unsatisfied with how much and how hard I have to work to get very little in return. From my family to my job, I need You, Father, to refocus my attention so I do not grow weary in well-doing.

I know it is written to leave an inheritance for my children, and I am working to do that, but it has been tough. When I feel unsatisfied, I also grow unmotivated. I am trying to see the point in what I am doing, but I struggle with finding my balance when the results are underwhelming. Father, help me to have realistic expectations also so if I am unsatisfied, it is not a problem with me.

I can be hard on myself and on others. I don't mean to be hard for no good reason. Show me how to motivate others so they, too, are not unsatisfied with my teaching, parenting, or leadership. Show me how to exceed expectations with balance. Teach me how to use my time wisely.

Show me how to find something to focus my attention on so when I feel unsatisfied, I can reflect on Your goodness. I can see what is going well and celebrate that if I cannot celebrate anything else. Teach me to be on top of what I must do to bring You glory and build my understanding.

I thank You, Father, for helping me to overcome being unsatisfied with my life, choices, family, and work. Remind me to be grateful today for what is good and allow that to be my motivation to keep pressing when I want to quit. Help me to see my hope, so I look beyond my experience and my current situation. In Yahshua's name, hallelujah and so be it."

# JOURNAL

## Share Your Thoughts or Answered Prayers

_____

_____

_____

_____

_____

_____

_____

_____

_____

_____

_____

_____

_____

_____

_____

_____

_____

_____

# PRAYER GREEDY

Greed is a sin that the Father hates. It is an unquenchable desire to have something and is often linked to a fear of poverty or lack that is spiraled out of control. It is a lust for finer things at the expense of your emotional, physical, and spiritual well-being. If greed is a problem in your life or someone you love, let us pray.

"Father, God above all things big and small. Thank You for hearing us today. Thank You for looking to earth, and being mindful of us, who are so small and limited in understanding. Teach us Your ways, oh God, so that we do not sin against You.

Father, I am asking You to expose the ways I am greedy. You teach us to have self-control, and in some ways, I am not. I am unbalanced, and I can see it. I know I have an unhealthy balance for working. I am set on working more than I enjoy my family.

I am focused on my greed to succeed or my hunger, when it was innocent, that now I am entrapped, and I don't know how to get off the wheel. I don't know how to jump off because everything is spinning, and I feel like I need more and more. But Father, You said, that destruction and hell are never full and the eyes of man are never satisfied.

When we are set on something that grows like a vein or cancer, and it shifts our focus because what was the initial intention gets left behind, greed can have an evil hand in our lives. It can guide us to believe our hard work is for the good and not for greed. We can try to get it all done in one day, when two or three days would not have cost our marriage or our children.

When the Hebrews had to go out of Egypt, the real trip could have taken 3 days, but the long trip took 40 years, and many did not make it at all! We can be greedy or lack focus and faith to accomplish what You send us out to do. Help us, Father, not to allow us to develop an unhealthy balance with work ethic.

Teach us to be balanced, oh God. Teach us to overindulge in food, in work, at the gym, to where we are sacrificing our health and quality of life for things temporal. Heal the places and situations that greed has attempted to destroy. Father, give us back what the enemy thought he stole from us in the name of Yahshua, amen."

# JOURNAL

## Share Your Thoughts or Answered Prayers

_____

_____

_____

_____

_____

_____

_____

_____

_____

_____

_____

_____

_____

_____

_____

_____

_____

_____

_____

_____

# PRAYER
## HATE

Hate is a strong word that has made it into our society. This rooted emotion, spirit even, is bred in every culture, race, ethnic group, and country. This spirit is unbiased, but it works to make us biased through hate. If you are overcome by hate or want to send it back to hell, let's pray.

"Father, You are a good God who knows and sees what we do not. You know the plans for righteous hatred and unholy hatred. I know You know the plans You have for us, but we can struggle to see it. Thank You for having a vision for Your creation! Thank You for being the Mighty Creator set on creating a people to bring You glory!

Thank You for looking past our colors, ethnic backgrounds, language barriers, and other things that are man-made to find a way to deliver us out of the snares of hatred and bigotry. Thank You, oh Mighty God, for being

Love, what the world needs more of now. Father, we are coming to You to break the yoke of hatred in our hearts, from our minds, in our children, our speech, and our thoughts and actions. May You have full reign in our lives to make us new creatures. Ones that see the world more and more like You, and less and less like the powers that surround us.

Give us the ability to see past the smokescreen that has put women against men. Children against their parents, and race against race. Help us to see that we are all Your creation and You have plans for us all. We all fall short of the glory of the Most High, no one is perfect, and we all have experiences that we could blame on all others who look or talk similarly.

Help us not to be biased because of physical makeup, but be discerners of spirit. Help us to see past the image and likeness, but deeper to reveal the spirit behind the man, woman, or child. We are to love the person but hate evil, our true enemy. We are at war not against flesh and blood, but the powers of darkness, systems, and evil spirits sent to seduce and manipulate humanity. We are sent into the world to deliver the lost ones by pointing them to The Truth, to Your Love, and Salvation.

Help us to do that without hatred. Help us to see lost souls as You do, Redeemable!

Thank You for what You have already done for me, which gives me hope! Help me to hate the plans of the enemy and for that not to turn to racism, sexism, or another bias. Father, we bind the spirit of hatred in Yahshua's name. We call out this evil spirit and the aftermath of its actions in the world.

We call out racism and expose that it is not sent from You. We pull down the doctrine, and we expose the liar. There are no super-beings except the ones endowed with Your Power. We are all fallible, we all make mistakes, we all need love, a place to live, food, water, and to rid ourselves of waste. We are all built this way, and we need our Creator to realign us today.

The chosen were not chosen to simply win and see everyone else losers. They were chosen to be the example and the teacher, priest, pastors, helps, prophets, singers, to bring lost souls to the Kingdom of God from every nation and tongue. Remind us today, it is not just about saving those in our churches, those who have a will to serve You and are conscious of You. But it is about going to places like Nineveh and bringing good news!

Going into highways and byways and showing that You love the unlovable. That You care for those who have made mistakes, who are murderers, rapist, devil worshipers, witches, warlocks, criminals, liars, deceivers, manipulators, victims, strippers, prostitutes, cheaters, thieves, the hurting, and the broken. You are the Savior who delivers us, and the Bible is evidence that no one is too hard or far gone for You to fix and mend.

May you remind us today, when we speak the words lost cause, Father, You said You would leave 99 to go and pursue the one. You said all of heaven rejoices when one comes back. We don't know which ones will return. We don't know how many will return, but Father, give us the heart to see the value in one—no matter their condition, race, country, language, or lifestyle, because Father, You rejoice when one You created comes into the knowledge and truth about You!

May we never forget our assignment and where our hate should lie. We should hate the things You hate. You said that 7 are an abomination: pride, lying, violence, evil scheming, eagerness to do wrong, false testimony, and sowing discord among brethren. You said that the ones practicing evil, which is sexual immorality, impurity, sensuality, idolatry, sorcery, enmity, strife, jealousy, fits of anger, rivalries, dissensions, divisions, envy, drunkenness, orgies, and things like these will not inherit the Kingdom of God.

Father, expose our love for these evil practices that have bewitched us. These attachments have us sinning against You and bringing out hate and not love, which is joy, peace, patience, kindness, goodness, faithfulness, gentleness, and self-control. Set us free today, Father.

Bind the enemies we cannot see, the evil spirits that plague our lives, and turn our hatred against evil to men, women, and children. Expose the liar now in Yahshua's name, and cast him down. Hallelujah and so be it!"

# JOURNAL

## Share Your Thoughts or
## Answered Prayers

_____

_____

_____

_____

_____

_____

_____

_____

_____

_____

_____

_____

_____

_____

_____

_____

_____

_____

_____

_____

# PRAYER SERVICE

The father said the strongest, best among men, are the ones who serve. If you are in a place of service, customer service, serving your family, society, the community, or people in need, that is a great position to be in. The Father blesses a cheerful giver! This prayer is a celebration of service but also a cry for those who desire to serve more. Join me.

"Father, You are a good giver! You give life, wisdom, hope, joy, friendship, love, and every other good thing. You said that all good things come from You! Father, we thank You for giving us good gifts today and showing us the acts of love and protection. Father, You loved us so much that You gave!

You sent Your Son to earth not to be worshiped, but to serve! He served Your Word and will, and went to the cross to fulfill Your plans for humanity. Thank You for Your bold act of service and love! May we return our gratitude by accepting the unimaginable gift and love You've shown, by serving others.

The Messiah washed the feet of the disciples in an act of love and service. May we not look at the dirt on others and assume we are too good to serve. May You bind this spirit of pride and send it back to hell from where it came from. May You bring humility into our lives, so that we don't groan at serving but find joy in it instead.

May we not turn our backs when it is time to give, give of our time, money, energy, or intellect. May we share love, the love that Christ is showing us. May we share the Good news we have out of an act of love and worship, service to the Almighty King! May we be good disciples called by Your name to bring good news to the world!

Father, help us to be more selfless. To put the needs of the Kingdom before our own. You said to seek first the Kingdom of God and Your righteousness, and You will add everything else unto us. When we give You our lives, that is when we find it. When we commit to serve You, that is when we receive gifts and rewards unimaginable.

You do things that have no words and are hard to understand because You Love us. Thank You, Father, for that today! Thank You for being mighty and strong in battle for us.

Thank You for Your angels that You send to serve Your purpose.

Thank You that not one word You speak will turn unto You void. You will use an animal, angel, human, spirit, or even the earth to accomplish Your plans! All things are at Your service! Father, help me to complete my reasonable service as Paul says, and serve You as a willing vessel, set on honoring and worshiping You through my service.

For those with a heart and track record of serving others, may You give them a double blessing now. May You fill their purse, enlarge their territory, and shower them with gifts and confidence. May Your mighty Hand show up for them and those they lead. May You bless their staff, business, and customers.

Please continue to bless the works of their hands, Father. Send them favor and blessings unimaginable. You said signs, miracles, and wonders will follow us, and we thank You for them now. In the name of Your Son, Yahshua, we say hallelujah and so be it!"

# JOURNAL

## Share Your Thoughts or Answered Prayers

_____

_____

_____

_____

_____

_____

_____

_____

_____

_____

_____

_____

_____

_____

_____

_____

_____

_____

_____

_____

_____

_____

# PRAYER SATISFIED

Being satisfied is when you have enough, and you don't need more. Sometimes, being satisfied is not enough, and we want more and more. But I want to encourage you, if you want a healthy balance with satisfaction, let's pray to expose what holds us back from it.

"Father, You are the holy one who knows what we need. You know how You fashioned our bodies and minds. You know the plans You have for us, and we trust that they are good. We know that Your plans are higher than ours, and we can be tempted to be satisfied with things, actions, people, or situations that You say are not enough or beneath us.

Father, stretch us today. Stretch our imagination if we are dreaming too small. Stretch our belief, if our faith is too small. Guide our hands as we work toward the mark. Direct our plans so that we finish what we start.

Build our confidence so we don't turn away what You said was meant to satisfy us. You said it is Your will to fill us up if we lack. If we lack wisdom, you will give it to us liberally when we ask. If we lack food, clothes, water, or shelter, You said You will provide for us out of Your riches to take care of us. If we are heavy in thought or think to worry, You tell us You will give us rest and peace.

You tell us to fear not, but many of us are struggling with some or all of this. Help us to be satisfied with Your Word of truth. Help us to see that Your word and Your promises are enough. You are more than enough, and You will not ever fail us. Father, guide us into all truth.

Help us not to develop a body or a consciousness that is greedy and will do anything to be stuffed. Gluttony is a sin when we eat past being satisfied. When work past satisfied, when we don't know how to follow Your Word and achieve balance, but we are in overdrive. This position causes loss in other areas, although we succeed in another.

Help us not to sacrifice one thing to get another if all the things are equally important. Teach us how not to lean on our own understanding but to trust You. Trust You when You say it is enough. When manna fell from the sky, You told Your people not to take more for tomorrow, but only for today. Those who thought to take for tomorrow, that food was rotten by the next day.

Some of us are storing up things that will be rotten when we think to eat them or use them because it was only provision for the day and not for the next day. Give us wisdom on how to be satisfied and not overindulge in anything. This too shall pass, is meant for the day, pain, things we like, and things we don't. Teach us balance and structure so we are free to enjoy all aspects of You and walk in the overflow! In Jesus name, amen!"

# JOURNAL

## Share Your Thoughts or
## Answered Prayers

_____

_____

_____

_____

_____

_____

_____

_____

_____

_____

_____

_____

_____

_____

_____

_____

_____

_____

_____

# PRAYER OVERFLOW

Walking in the overflow is where we all may desire to be. A place of abundance and more than enough, for many, this might sound like a dream. But there is a way to experience the overflow. Which is to walk in power and boldness.

"Father, You are the God of More than an enough. You are the one who holds all things and all people in Your Hand. You have plans for our lives, ones we can trust and lean on. Father, I thank You for helping us to see the big picture today. To know that we are walking in the overflow, this is when we are fully saturated with Your Presence, Word, and Love.

Father, we thank You for Your Presence and active guidance in our lives. Thank You for getting us to a point where we can trust Your decisions and will for our lives. Thank You for directing us out of the abyss and reminding us to reach for You. Thank You for Your Word, the word that is a light to our feet and keeps us on the path.

We don't live in fear because we know that no matter the test, You are here with us. No matter what comes, You will help me to fight my battles. You will never leave me nor forsake me. Father, thank You for Your Love. This gives me the confidence to know that I am loved, and no matter if I make mistakes, I have You to pull me through.

You will turn things for my good. If I suffer awhile, I know that joy will come in the morning. I don't allow bad situations to bring on depression because You are my hope. You keep me in a state of balance. When life happens, I smile, because what is happening around me is not the center of my joy– You are.

Thank You for bringing people in my life and for the good days where things just flow. For the good seasons where everything is working to my good and I can see it. But also, Father, thank You for the times where I have to work harder. Thank You for putting me in a place of overflow, which builds confidence, balance, love, and eternal joy. Thank You for the peace that comes in this place because I am aware and assured that all things are working for my good and the good of those who love

You.

Father, continue to keep me and us in Your plan. Thank You for finishing the work You started in me. Thank You, Father, for the overflow that will run from my life and encourage others. Thank You for helping me to show it to my family and those I meet. Help me to smile through trouble and be a marvel for how things turn to my good.

Allow me to be a sign, miracle, and a wonder to all who see me and my life, to say, "Wow, look at God!" Father, You are so good, and You have been better than good to me, and I thank You!"

# JOURNAL

## Share Your Thoughts or Answered Prayers

_____

_____

_____

_____

_____

_____

_____

_____

_____

_____

_____

_____

_____

_____

_____

_____

_____

_____

_____

_____

# ABOUT THE AUTHOR

*"God blesses those who work for peace, for they will be called the children of Yah (God)."* Matthew 5:9

Dr. Lee has authored over fifty books across more than seven genres: adult, children, youth fiction, self-help, spiritual growth, novels, business, empowerment, etc. to help people in their most profound times of need.

She is also passionate about coaching programs and web courses she created for WAE (Write Anything Easily) Process, Embrace Your Crown, Turn Key Solution for Small and New Businesses, Transform Go Beyond Change (Personal Development, and The Lesson for youth and teenagers.

Connect and Shop my books:

AuthorKLee.com

# A CALL TO
## PRAY GLOSSARY

# A Call to
# PRAY

| VOL. 1 | VOL. 2 |
|---|---|
| SALVATION | FORGIVENESS |

# A Call to
# PRAY

## VOL. 3
## SABBATH

1. Fill Me
2. Bitterness
3. Hopeful
4. Joy
5. Increase
6. Wisdom
7. Discernment
8. Laziness
9. Freedom
10. Disappointment
11. Excitement
12. Depression
13. Addiction
14. Food
15. Daily Routine
16. Thankful
17. Spiritual Warfare
18. Witchcraft
19. Delay
20. Jail
21. Failure
22. Beauty
23. Selfish
24. Narcissist
25. Hard Headed
26. Business
27. Dreams
28. Goals
29. Achievement
30. Insecure

## VOL. 4
## FASTING

1. Friendship
2. Pregnancy
3. Abortion
4. Guidance
5. Growth
6. Academics
7. Protection
8. Providing
9. Humility
10. Multitasking
11. Purity
12. Charity
13. Endurance
14. Spiritual Understanding
15. Time
16. Comfort
17. Hospitality
18. Judgment
19. Legal
20. Decision Making
21. Wellbeing
22. Stress
23. Anxiety
24. Comparison
25. Affection
26. Wisdom
27. Worrying
28. Doubt
29. Deliverance
30. Repentance

# A Call to
# PRAY

## VOL. 5
### FRUITS

1. Lying
2. Stealing
3. Self Control
4. Empowerment
5. Obedience
6. Suicide
7. Reverence
8. Mercy
9. Grace
10. Glory
11. Kingdom of God
12. Dependability
13. Interdependence
14. Justify
15. Favoritism
16. Perception
17. Holiness
18. Forgiveness
19. Isolation
20. Mutilation
21. Success
22. Patience
23. Hell
24. Heaven
25. Healing
26. Generosity
27. Proximity
28. Future
29. Past
30. Communication

## VOL. 6
### LOVE

1. Trust
2. Invitation
3. Welcome
4. Gratitude
5. Birthday
6. Christmas
7. Resurrection Sunday
8. Palm Sunday
9. Passover
10. Youth
11. Groups
12. Inclusion
13. Choice
14. Forgetful
15. Memory
16. Nutrition
17. Favor
18. Needs
19. Faithful
20. Reliable
21. Hear
22. Perfectionist
23. Teachable
24. Honesty
25. Secrets
26. Embarrassment
27. Public Speaking
28. Example
29. Flesh
30. Distractions

# A Call to
# PRAY

## VOL. 7
## BEATITUDES

1. Decoys
2. Good
3. Vessel
4. Believer
5. Empty
6. Victory
7. Contentment
8. Respect
9. Mission
10. Purpose
11. Patterns
12. Familiar Spirits
13. Mistakes
14. Lessons
15. Stingy
16. Giving
17. Gifts
18. Abundance
19. Word
20. Eternal Life
21. Disobedient
22. Pleasure
23. Experience
24. Music
25. Unsatisfied
26. Greedy
27. Hate
28. Service
29. Satisfied
30. Overflow

## VOL. 8
## VANITY

1. Expectation
2. Insufficient
3. Law
4. Law Breaker
5. Homosexual
6. Keeping
7. Righteousness
8. Bragging
9. Liar
10. Position
11. Anointing
12. Reputation
13. Authority
14. Attracting
15. Born Again
16. Holy Spirit
17. Crying
18. Hurt
19. Dedication
20. Fake
21. Hold
22. Controlling
23. Marginalization
24. Fear
25. Torment
26. Imperfection
27. Thoughts
28. Understanding
29. Regeneration
30. Inquity

# A Call to
# PRAY

## VOL. 9
### CHARACTER

## VOL. 10
### CROSS

# A Call to
# PRAY

## VOL. 11
### REDEMPTION

1. Immorality
2. Leader
3. Guide
4. Mentor
5. Preach
6. Spiritual Gifts
7. Testimony
8. Subjection
9. Guilty
10. King of Kings
11. Sovereignty
12. Justified
13. Godly Sorrow
14. Shame
15. Bring Up the Past
16. Equality
17. Government
18. Community
19. The Body of Christ
20. Confirmation
21. Show Me
22. Restoration
23. Powerless
24. Assurance
25. Loyalty
26. Interruption
27. Pride
28. Prejudice
29. Travel
30. Stagnation

## VOL. 12
### FREE

1. Loss
2. Barren
3. New Day
4. Name Calling
5. Denial
6. Gluttony
7. Blasphemy
8. Jealousy
9. Envy
10. Lust
11. Violence
12. Manipulation
13. Rivalry
14. Unfair
15. Covet
16. Idols
17. Honor Your Parents
18. Priority
19. Mind Your Words
20. Do What I am Told
21. Offense/Offended
22. Ego
23. Household
24. Social Norms
25. Narrative
26. Perception
27. Second Guessing
28. When I Am Wrong
29. Considerate
30. Hard Working

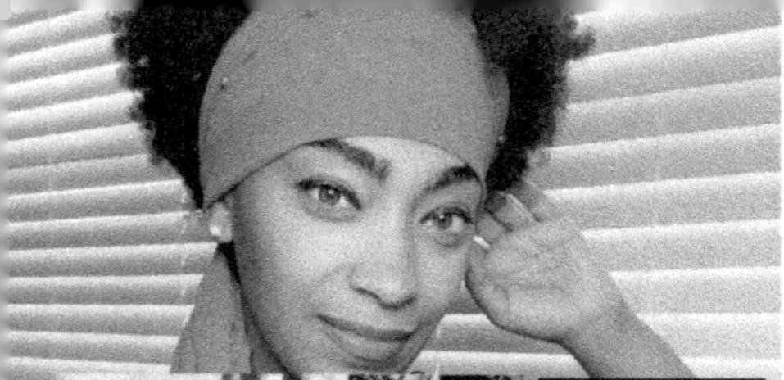

*Order*
**Books!**

**AuthorKLee.com Creator of *WAE Proces***

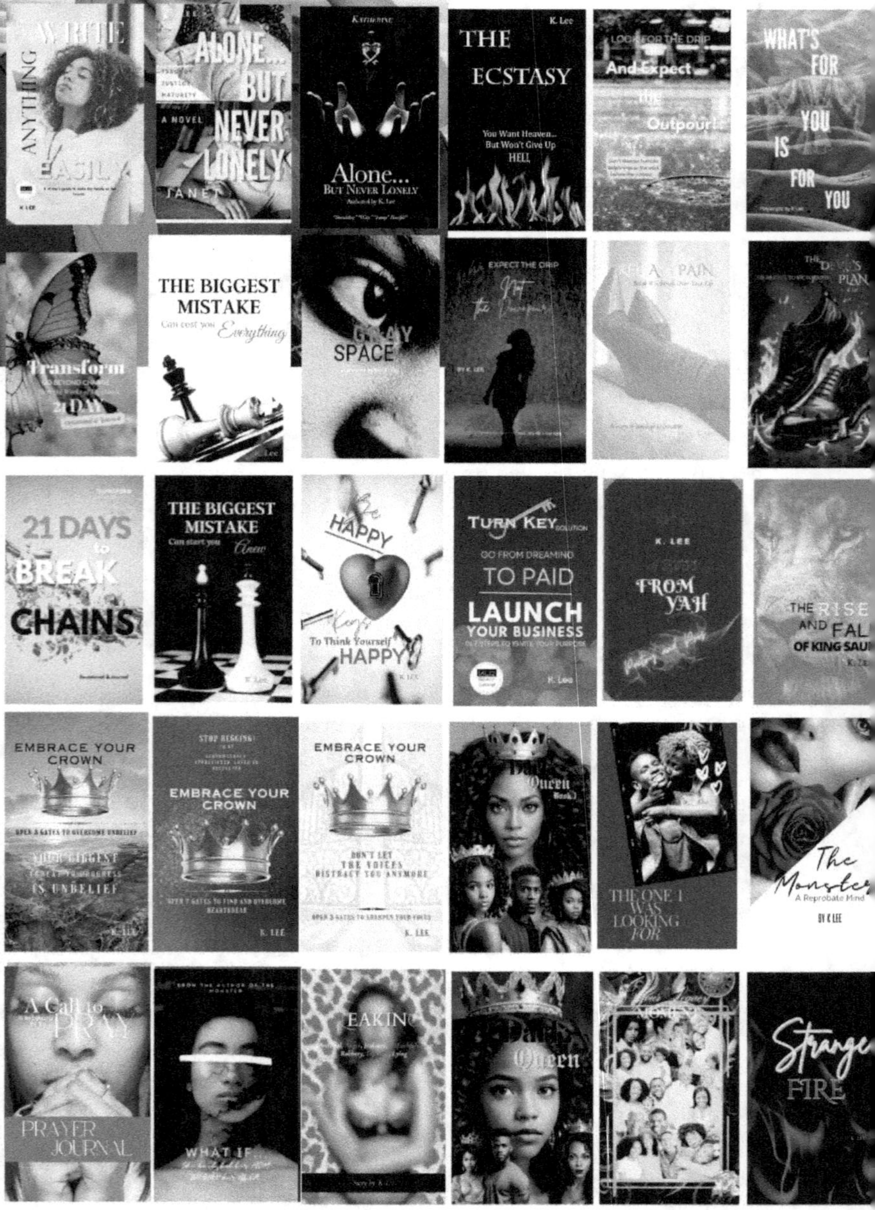

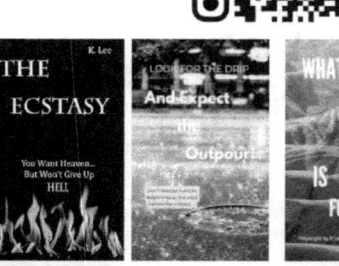

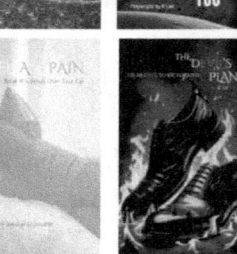

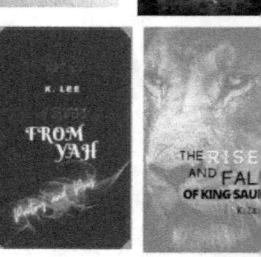

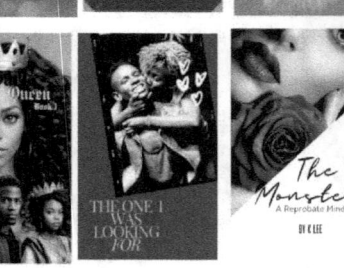

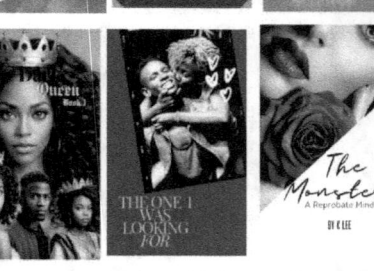

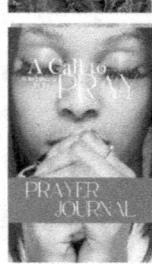

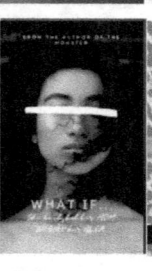

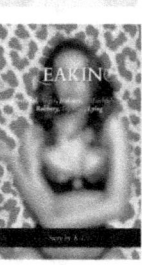

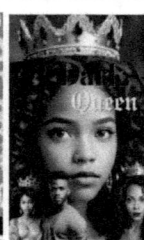

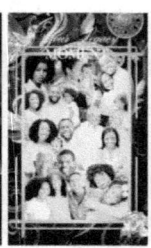

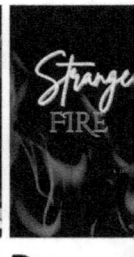

# Explore over seven different book genres, and find something suitable for every member of the family.

# SCAN ME

**Call or Text:**
**770-240-0089 Press Extension 1**
**Web: KLEpub.com**
**Email Services@klepub.com**

It's time to start and finish **YOUR Story**!

KLE Publishing specializes in helping people become authors. In as little as 15 to 90 days, we can help you develop your books and e-books and publish to 39,000 outlets! We also offer audiobook services.

**Write, Edit, Format, Publish**
We can help from
**Start to Finish.**

# Explore and learn more about published authors affiliated with KLE.

# KLEPub.com

## A Prayer of Thanks

Father, I would like to thank You for blessing every person who has determined to pick up this book, e-book, or audiobook and share it with someone. May You bless them richly and help them through life using the prayers in this series, but also through the prayer life they are building with You. May they make praying a habit that will last a lifetime. In Yahshua's name, amen.

## A Prayer of Blessing

Father, I would like to ask you to bless the families, businesses, organizations, countries, and special donors who have a heart to answer this call to pray. May you bless them and give them a prophet's reward for their faithfulness. May they understand that not one penny they invested into this vision will be wasted, but all of it will bless the Kingdom and work as good seed. Father, You said that You would give seed to the sower, may You bless them with more seed to sow more wherever they go. In the name that is above every name, Yahshua, Jesus the Christ, we pray and say thank You; so be it!"